Accidental Genius

Science Puzzles for Clever Kids

PLANETS, SPACESHIPS, MOONS, and STARS

Alix Wood

WINDMILL BOOKS

Published in 2023 by Windmill Books,
an Imprint of Rosen Publishing
29 East 21st Street, New York, NY 10010

Written and designed by Alix Wood

Printed in the United States of America

CPSIA Compliance Information: Batch CSWM23: For Further Information contact Rosen Publishing, New York, New York at 1-800-237-9932

Cataloging-in-Publication Data

Names: Wood, Alix.
Title: Planets, spaceships, moons, and stars / Alix Wood.
Description: New York : Windmill Publishing, 2023. | Series: Accidental genius: science puzzles for clever kids
Identifiers: ISBN 9781508198895 (pbk.) | ISBN 9781508198901 (library bound) | ISBN 9781508198918 (ebook)
Subjects: LCSH: Puzzles--Juvenile literature. | Picture puzzles--Juvenile literature. | Games--Juvenile literature. | Outer space--Juvenile literature. | Space ships--Juvenile literature. | Moon--Juvenile literature.
Classification: LCC GV1493.W66 2023 | DDC 793.73--dc23

Contents

The Solar System

Our sun and its planets are known as the solar system. Planets are enormous, ball-shaped objects that travel around the sun. There are eight planets in our solar system. We live on Earth.

Can you answer these planet questions?

1) Which planet is the largest?

2) Which planet is very windy?

3) Look at the picture. Which planet is closest to the sun?

Can you find the eight planets in this word search?

MERCURY
VENUS
EARTH
MARS
JUPITER
SATURN
URANUS
NEPTUNE

M	W	A	K	T	O	M	Y	M	P
J	I	P	N	U	R	A	A	E	M
U	S	Q	E	T	R	U	R	R	E
P	W	A	P	T	Y	U	M	C	S
I	S	E	T	U	S	O	N	U	P
T	F	A	U	U	P	L	H	R	T
E	P	J	N	T	R	T	M	Y	S
R	W	A	E	H	R	N	O	L	A
H	R	X	O	A	Y	U	G	R	E
U	W	Q	E	T	V	E	N	U	S

Night and Day

Planets spin as they travel around the sun. As Earth spins, the side that faces the sun is lit up. The other side is dark. That is why we have day and night.

Look where the sun is shining.
Is it day or night where the dots are?
Choose the right answer.

1)

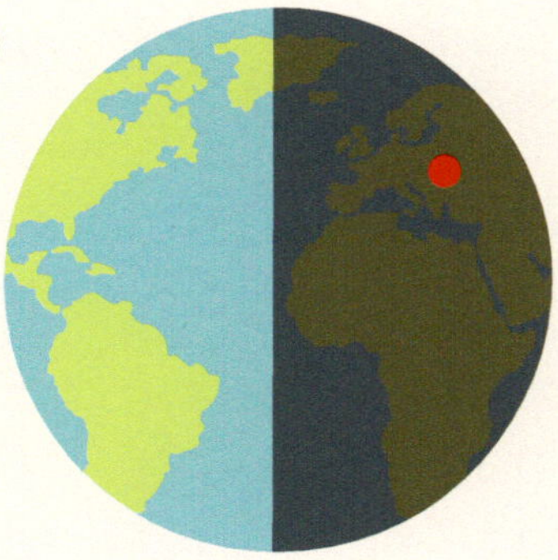

day | night

2)

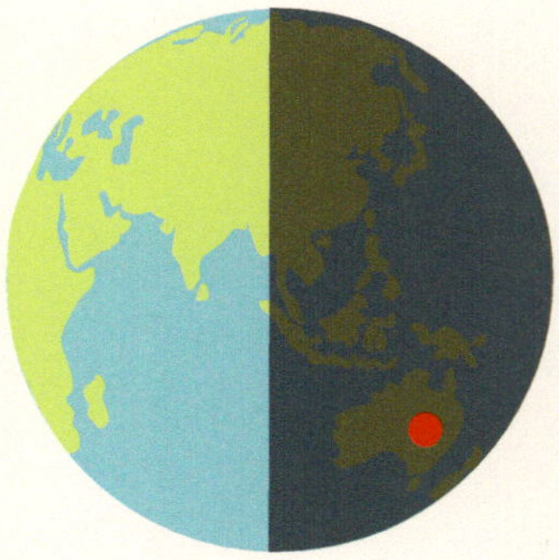

day | night

3)

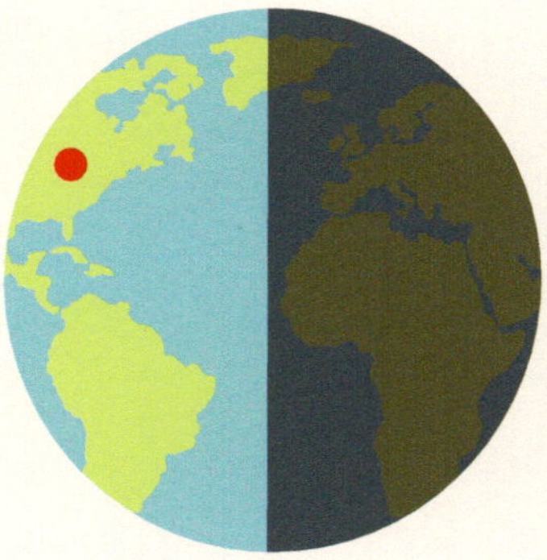

day | night

4)

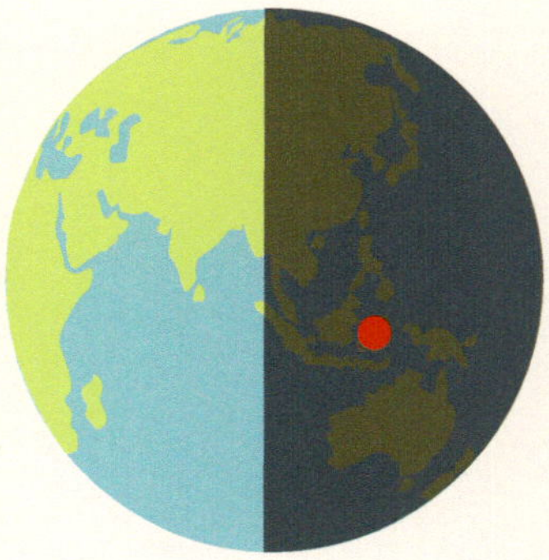

day | night

Understand Night and Day

You will need: a ball, a flashlight, and a dark place.

1. In a dark place, hold the ball in one hand. Shine the flashlight onto the ball.
2. Slowly turn the ball around. The side that was lit up is now in darkness. The side that was dark is now lit.

Did you know?
The icy North and South Poles are always farthest from the sun's rays as Earth spins around.

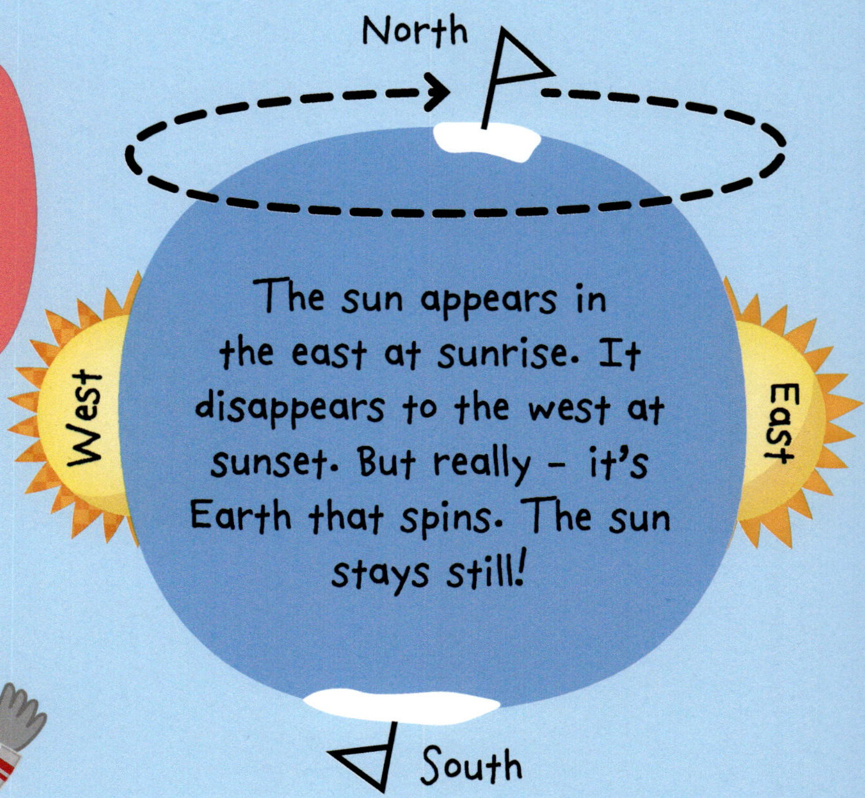

Can you finish this sentence?

The sun rises in the _ _ _ _.

North	South	East	West

The Goldilocks Planet

Do you know the story "Goldilocks and the Three Bears?" In the story, Goldilocks tries the three bears' porridge. Papa Bear's porridge was too hot. Mama Bear's was too cold. But Baby Bear's porridge was just right.

Earth is called a Goldilocks planet, because it is just the right distance from the sun for us to live! Planets close to the sun, like Mercury, get too hot. Planets far from the sun, like Neptune, are too cold.

Can you match the words to the right bowl and planet?

too cold	too hot	just right

A thin layer of gases around Earth helps protect it from getting too hot or too cold. Imagine you are the sun's rays. Can you find your way through the gassy atmosphere to reach Earth?

Water and Air

It is not only the "just right" temperature that allows living things to survive on Earth. Earth has two other important things. It has enough good air to breathe, and it has water. We need water to drink and grow food. Some animals live in water.

Point to any creature that spends all or most of its time in the water.

Walrus

Lion

Hippopotamus

Dolphin

Alligator

Clown fish

Toucan

Jellyfish

Scientists get excited when they find any water or ice on a planet. It means that planet may support life!

Copy and Color!

Around 70 percent of Earth's surface is covered by water!

1. On your copy, color the oceans and seas blue.
2. Color the cooler land green.
3. Color the hot deserts yellow.
4. Leave the land near the cold North Pole white.

Our Eight Planets

The eight planets in our solar system are all very different. The planets closest to the sun are rocky. The faraway planets are mostly made of gas.

Color It In

Match each name to its planet. Use the sentence above to help you.

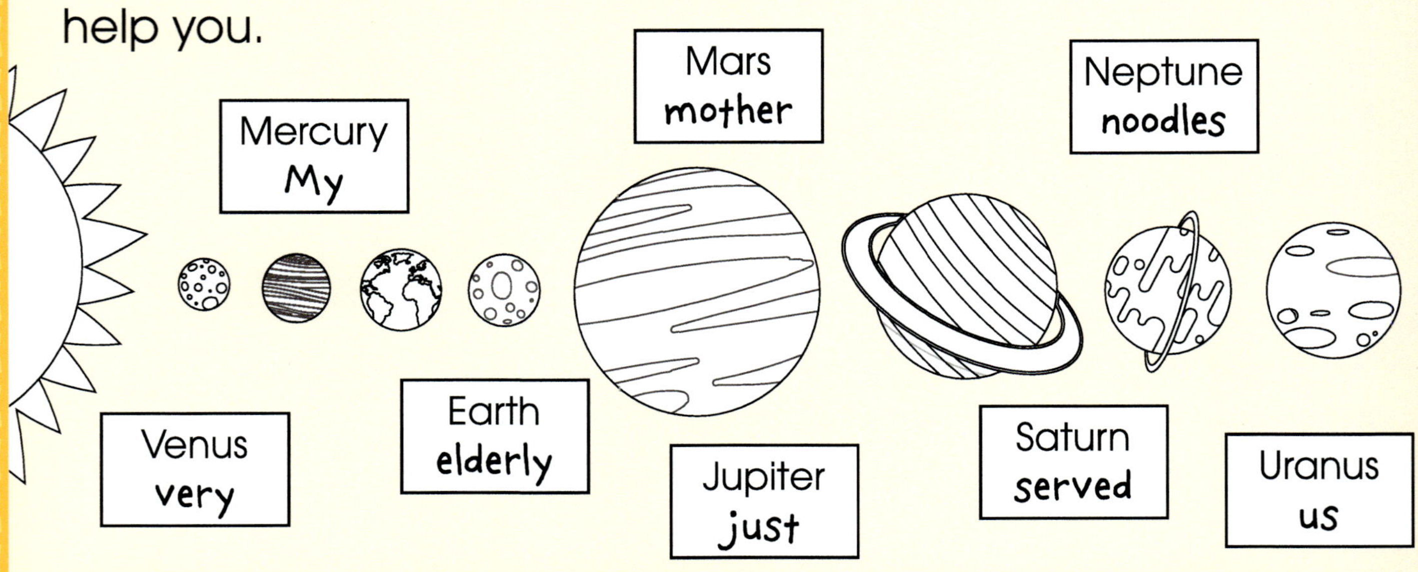

Some planets are big. Some planets are small. Can you number the planets from 1 for the smallest to 8 for the biggest?

There used to be nine planets in our solar system. The ninth planet was Pluto. In 2006, astronomers decided Pluto was too small to be called a planet!

Stars

Look up at the sky on a clear, dark night. What can you see? There are countless stars out in space. Stars are giant, bright balls of very hot gas. The nearest star to Earth is the sun.

Stars often come in pairs that travel around each other. Can you find four pairs of stars?

Did you know that stars are so far away it takes millions of years for their light to reach our eyes? The starlight you see at night is from stars that shone long ago.

Word Jumble

Each circle of letters is a jumbled-up word. Copy the jumbles below. Figure out each word. Then draw a line from each letter to the next letter, then from the last letter back to the first. What have you drawn?

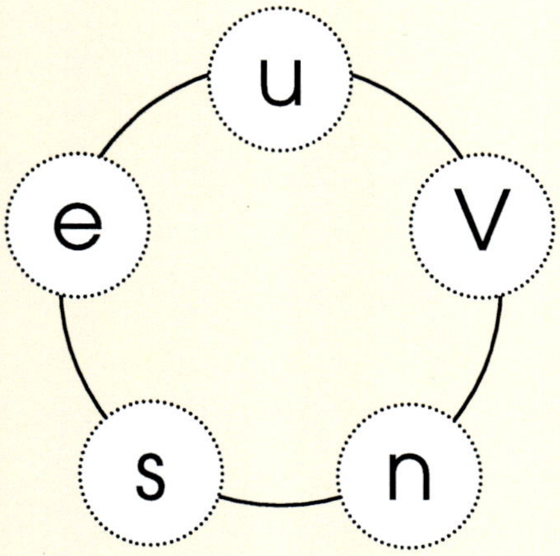

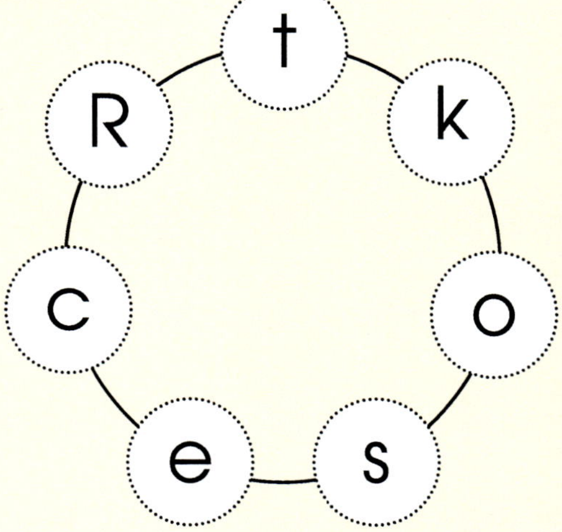

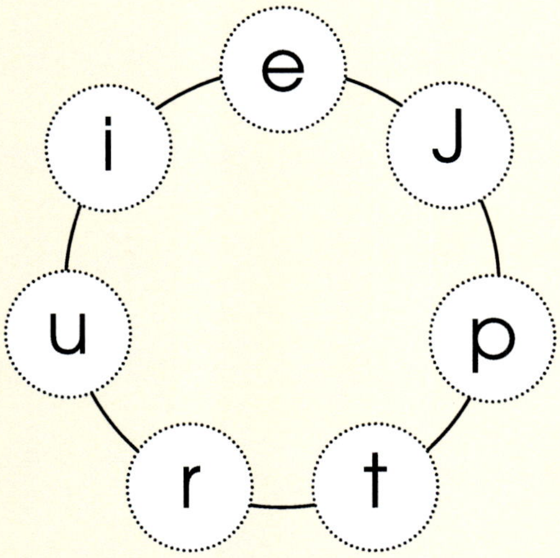

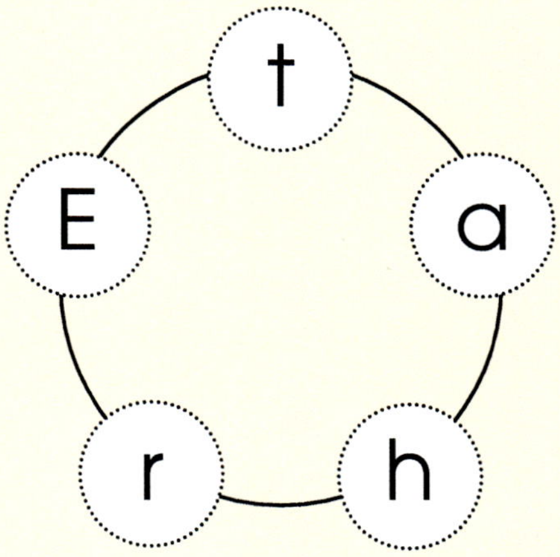

Clue – All the words have something to do with space.

Stars are really ball-shaped. They look twinkly because the starlight bends as it travels through the moving air.

Star Pictures

The night sky is like a giant connect-the-dots! Long ago, people looking at the stars made shapes from them. Stars that form patterns are called constellations.

Try it! What shapes can you see when you look at the stars at night?

This star pattern is called "the Big Dipper" because it looks like a ladle!

A Constellation Viewer

You will need: dark paper, toilet paper tube, tape, a thumbtack, a flashlight.

1. Tape a circle of the paper over the end of the tube.
2. Using a thumbtack, poke a hole where you want each star.
3. Hold the tube up to the light to see your constellation.

Tip: Project your constellation onto a wall by shining a flashlight through the tube.

This constellation is called Orion. Orion was a hunter. Copy the picture, then join the dots to see what he is holding.

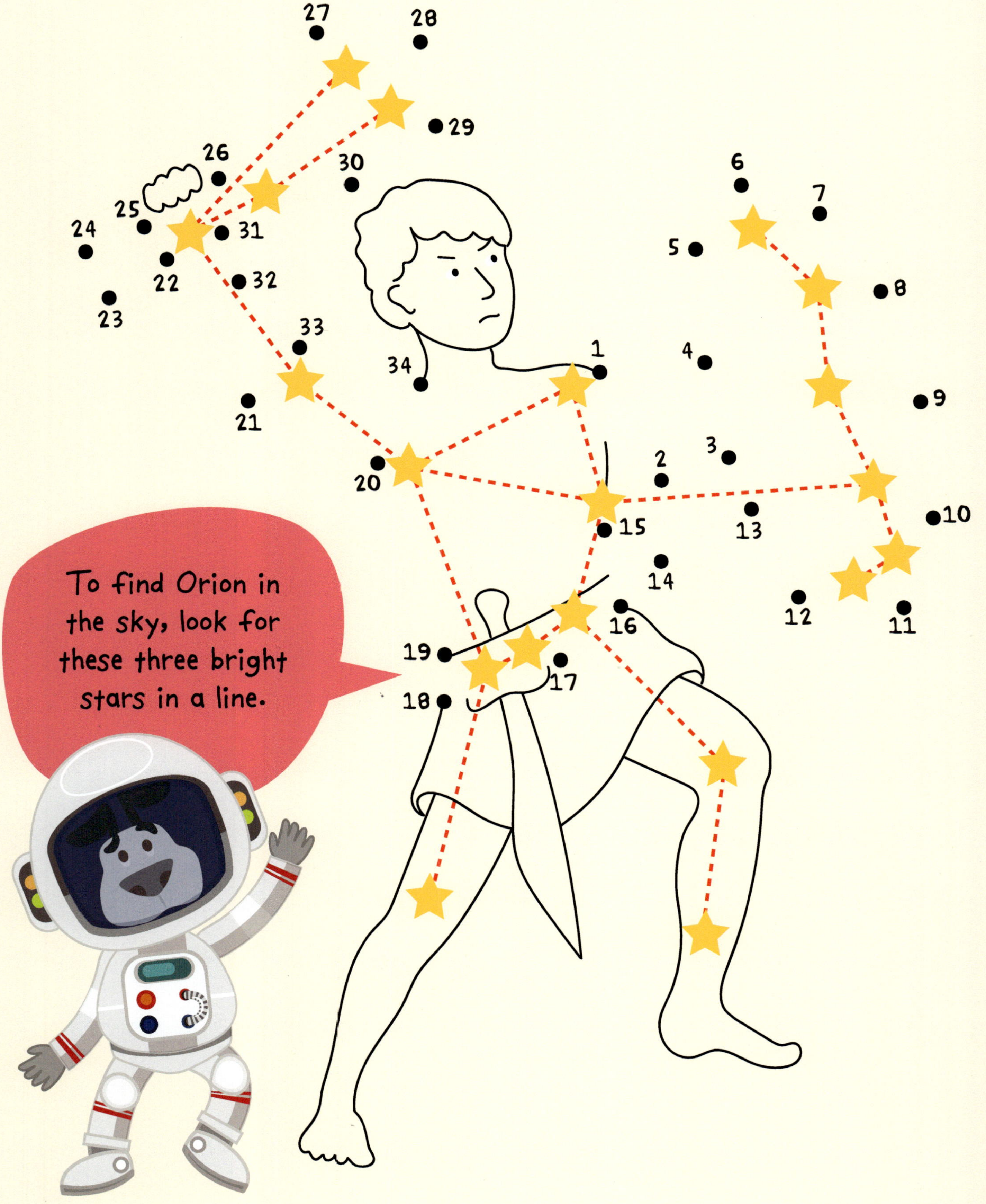

Our Big, Bright Sun

The sun is our brightest star. In the daytime it shines so brightly that we can't see any other stars! It is so bright you must never look straight at the sun. It can harm your eyes.

Did you know the sun can tell you around what time it is? That's because as Earth spins, the sun always appears to rise in the east and set in the west.

When the sun is high in the sky, it is around midday.

When the sun is low in the west, it is evening.

If the sun is low in the sky in the east, it must be early morning.

Find out which direction is east and est, and try it yourself.

Sunlight Starlight Experiment

You will need: your constellation viewer from page 16, a flashlight, a dark room with a bright light.

1. In a dark room, shine your flashlight through the constellation viewer. Can you see stars on the wall?
2. Now switch on the room's main light. Can you see the stars now?

What happened? The main room light is like our sun. It is so bright it drowns out the light from the other stars.

Space Rocks and Snowballs!

There are millions of lumps of ice, metal, and rock traveling around in space.

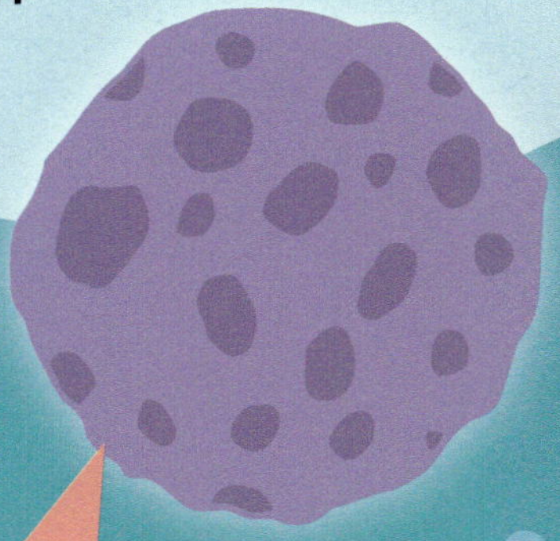

Asteroids are made of rock or metal. They are smaller than planets.

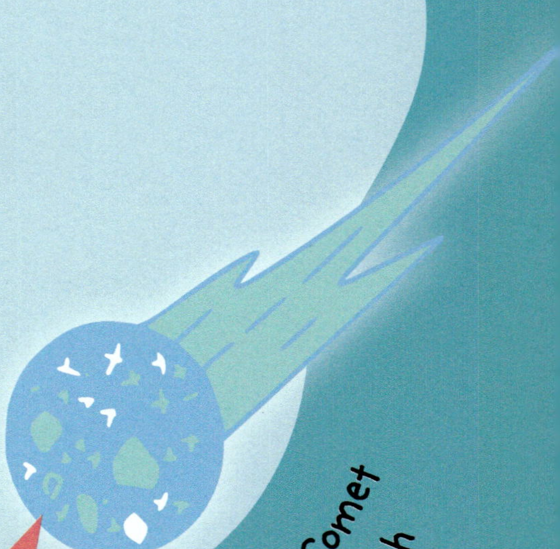

Comets are made of ice, dust, and rock. Near the hot sun their ice turns into a gas and forms a tail.

Halley's Comet passes Earth every 76 years.

Meteoroids are small pieces of rock or metal, often broken off an asteroid or comet.

If a meteoroid enters Earth's atmosphere, it heats up and begins to burn!

Burning meteoroids are known as meteors, or shooting stars.

Can you answer these questions?

1) Is an asteroid bigger than a planet? Yes No

2) Are comets made partly of ice? Yes No

3) Is a meteor a burning meteoroid? Yes No

4) What's another name for a meteor?

_   _ _ _ _ _ _ _ _   _ _ _ _

Cross-out Puzzle

What's that in the sky? Take out any letters that appear twice in the grid below. On separate paper, write each letter that only appears once. Can you make a word out of those letters?

R	W	A	E	P
F	C	I	N	L
U	I	N	R	S
P	W	A	O	F
M	S	L	T	U

The Milky Way

Our group of planets is part of the Milky Way galaxy. A galaxy is an enormous group of stars, gas, and dust. There are billions of different galaxies in space.

The Milky Way is a spiral galaxy. Which arm of the spiral has the most yellow stars, A or B?

Scientists use powerful telescopes to see faraway objects. Copy the grid below, then draw what you see in each individual square into the correct square on your grid. What can this telescope see?

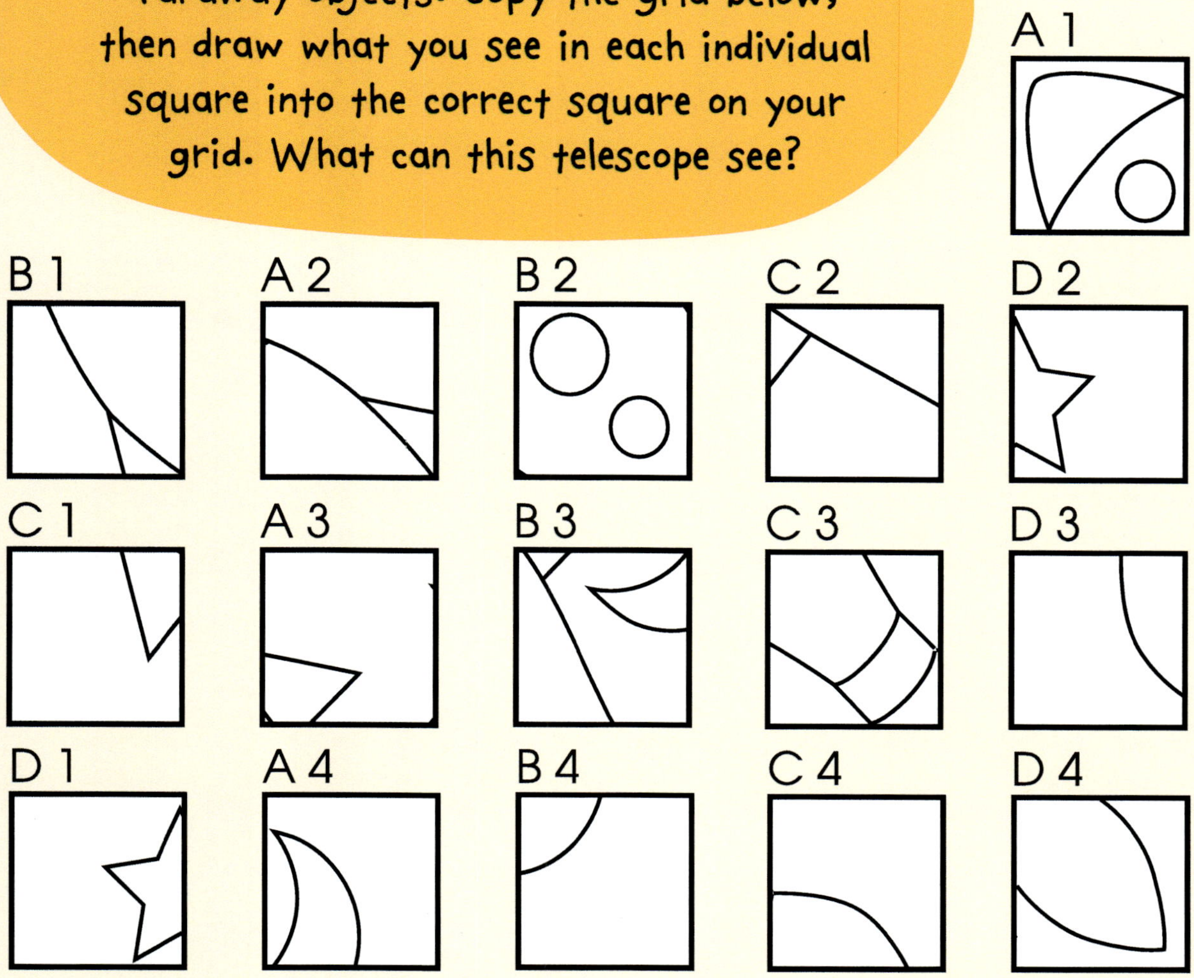

We have filled in the first square for you.

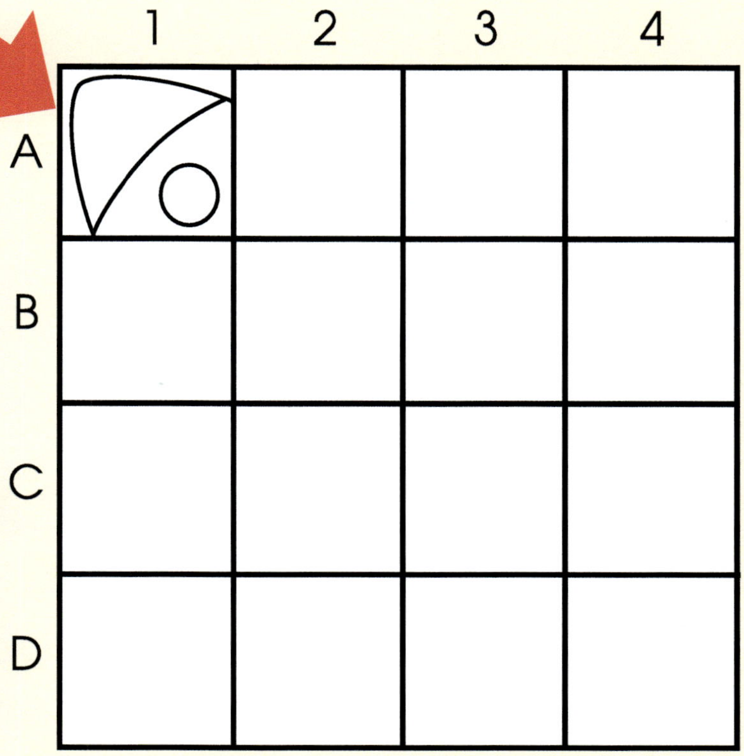

All About Gravity

When you throw a ball in the air, it doesn't zoom off into space. It comes back down again. Why? Gravity! Gravity is an invisible force that pulls things toward the center of massive objects. Earth's gravity pulls the smaller moon so it circles around it. Sun's gravity pulls Earth so it travels around the sun!

If Earth didn't have gravity, everything would float away! Can you spot 10 differences in these two pictures? A change in Earth's gravity has made things move, or disappear!

Rocket into Space

Space rockets need to be powerful to escape the pull of Earth's gravity. Rockets have big fuel tanks to help them travel fast enough and far enough. The fuel tanks are very heavy.

Make a Balloon Rocket

You will need: a drinking straw, a balloon, a long piece of string, tape, two chairs, a clothespin

1. Thread the string through the straw. How? Hold the straw upright and drop the string though, using the power of gravity!
2. Tie each end of the string to a chair.
3. Arrange the chairs so the string is taut.
4. Blow up the balloon. Hold the airhole closed using the clothespin.
5. Tape the balloon to the straw.
6. Slide the balloon to the chair at the airhole end.
7. Open the clothespin and watch your rocket zoom!

The escaping air pushes the balloon in the opposite direction! Rockets work in the same way. Gas escaping fast from the engine pushes the rocket upward. Your balloon rocket gets smaller, too, as it uses up its fuel!

To make your balloon look more like a space rocket, draw on it using a marker.

Do Aliens Exist?

No one knows. People have seen unusual objects in the sky. Could they be alien spaceships? Scientists believe aliens would have to come from other Goldilocks planets, far away.

Excitingly, scientists have discovered some possible planets! They are too far from Earth for us to explore yet, though.

Help the alien UFOs find their way back to the right planet.

UFO stands for "unidentified flying object."

Can you find these objects in this picture?

10 stars	**3** aliens
5 planets	**2** astronauts
4 UFOs	**1** space rocket

The Seasons

Our spinning Earth takes a year to travel around the sun. Did you know Earth spins slightly on its side? Because of this, different parts of the world lean toward the sun more at some times of the year. That's why we get different seasons!

Word Scramble

Unscramble the jumbled words to find the names of the four seasons.

1) PINSGR

2) REMMUS

3) LLAF

4) ITNWER

Countries on the top of Earth are leaning toward the sun. They get more hours of sunlight, so it is summer here.

The darker half gets less sunlight. It is winter there.

Now these countries lean toward the sun. So now it's summer here!

Can you match the picture to the season?

Winter

Spring

Summer

Fall

Gas Giants, Ice Giants

Four planets, Jupiter, Saturn, Uranus, and Neptune, are known as the "gas giants." They are really big and covered in gases! Uranus and Neptune are also called Ice Giants. They are very cold. Jupiter is our biggest planet. It is covered in swirling, stormy clouds.

Help the alien find its landing pad through the swirling gases of Jupiter!

Then, find the exit!

Jupiter Fun Facts

A year is how long it takes a planet to go around the sun. It takes Jupiter 11.8 Earth years to travel around the sun.

A day on Jupiter is only 10 hours long! An Earth day is 24 hours long.

Jupiter has at least 79 moons!

Even though it is a long way from Earth, Jupiter is so big you can see it without a telescope!

Jupiter is as wide as 11 Earths side by side!

Quiz Time!

1. How many moons does Jupiter have?

   a) just 1 moon b) at least 79 c) 7 moons

2. True or false? A day on Jupiter is shorter than a day on Earth.

   a) true b) false

Icy Dwarf Planets

Around the edge of our solar system there is a circle of icy rocks. Some of the rocks are dwarf planets. The circle is called the Kuiper Belt. It is very, very cold here. It is a long way from the sun.

Pluto was named by an eleven-year-old girl, Venetia Burney. She named it after the Roman god Pluto, who could make himself invisible.

Cross-out Puzzle

Take out any letters that appear twice in the grid below. On separate paper, write each letter that only appears once. Unscramble them to find the dwarf planet.

L	A	S	O	F
H	W	I	R	T
F	P	A	N	G
I	R	M	W	M
G	N	U	H	S

Shape Match

Match the dwarf planet shape to the correct name.

Eris

Haumea

Arrokoth

Astronauts

People who go to space are called astronauts. Before astronauts go to space they have to learn the skills they will need to survive. They learn to control the spacecraft and practice living with very little gravity.

Word Search

Find seven things astronauts need in space.

SPACESUIT
AIR
SPACESHIP
FOOD
DRINK
SLEEP
EXERCISE

U	L	S	J	Z	O	W	Y	H	E
L	E	P	N	S	L	E	E	P	T
E	S	A	E	T	C	U	R	O	K
P	X	C	F	B	Y	U	D	N	E
F	S	E	T	W	S	O	I	U	K
O	D	S	R	U	P	R	H	R	L
O	P	H	N	C	D	T	M	T	S
D	W	I	M	H	I	N	E	A	O
B	S	P	A	C	E	S	U	I	T
U	L	Q	U	T	V	E	E	R	S

Photocopy this page. Then draw and color what these astronauts can see though their spacecraft window.

The Moon

Our moon is a ball of rock that travels around Earth. It looks as if it shines, but it doesn't. Moonlight is actually sunlight shining onto the moon and bouncing off. Other planets have moons too.

It takes a month for the moon to travel all around the Earth.

Have you noticed that the moon seems to change shape? It doesn't really. As it moves around Earth some parts are lit by the sun and some are in shadow.

Moon Watch

Look at the moon on one evening every week. Shade an area of a circle each week to draw the shape of your moon. Watch the shape change.

Week 1 Week 2 Week 3 Week 4

Astronauts have walked on the moon! It took over three days to get there, traveling at super fast rocket speeds!

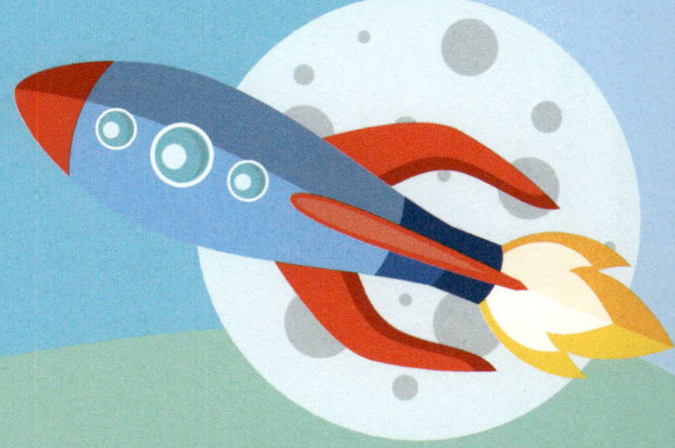

This astronaut is on the moon. What is he holding? Photocopy the picture, then join the dots to find out.

The Asteroid Belt

Between the planets Mars and Jupiter there is a swirling circle of rocky asteroids. This area is known as the asteroid belt. Sometimes, Jupiter's gravity pulls an asteroid toward Earth. The asteroid turns into a burning hot meteor!

Can you fly your spaceship safely through the asteroid belt? You must not go past any meteors! Pick up ten stars on the way.

Machines in Space

There are lots of machines in space. There are thousands and thousands of human-made satellites! We use them for our phone signals and internet. Some satellites photograph space or check the weather. Machines sometimes get left behind from space voyages, too.

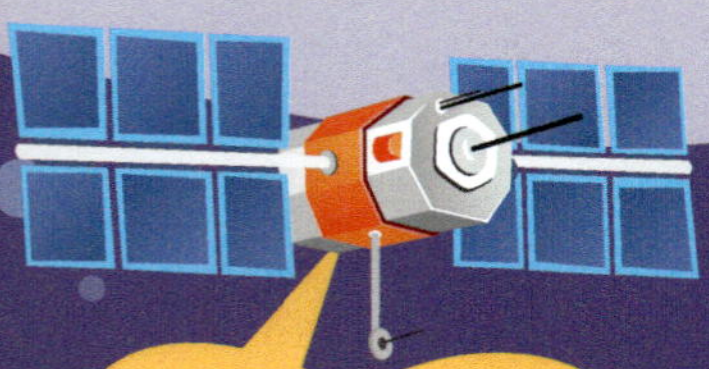

This satellite camera can study and photograph space.

Communication satellites send phone signals around the world.

The International Space Station is an enormous human-made satellite. Astronauts live on it.

Several moon rovers have been left behind on the moon!

Shape Match

Can you match each space machine shape to the right name?

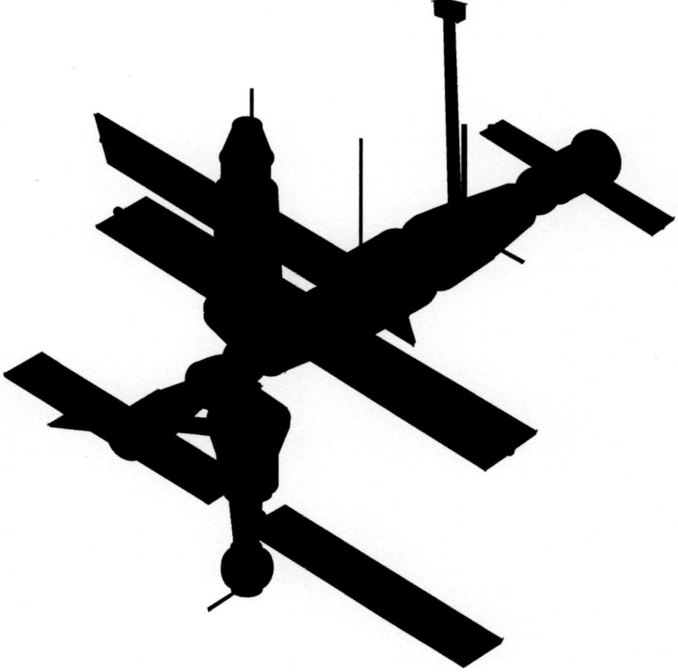

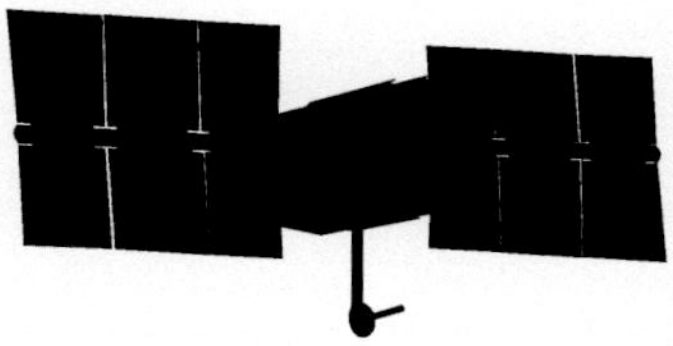

Communication Satellite

Satellite Camera

Moon Rover

Space Station

Spot the Space Station

The space station is the third brightest object in the night sky. You don't need a telescope to see it. Check the NASA or ESA website to see when it will fly over your house. It looks like a fast-moving star. It always appears from the west and heads east.

Space Genius Test

Are you a space genius? Answer these space questions to find out.

1 What is gravity?

a) A special sauce that astronauts eat

b) A bright star

c) An invisible force that pulls things to the center of planets

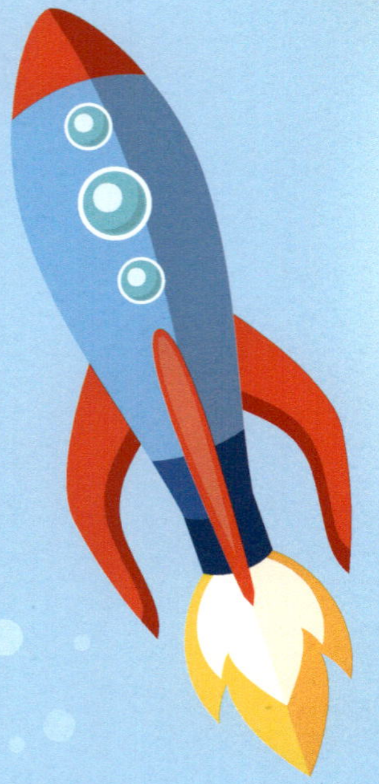

2 Which of these is true?

a) Moonlight is actually sunlight bouncing off the moon.

b) The moon is made of cheese.

c) No one has ever walked on the moon.

3 Our eight planets are Mercury, Venus, Earth, Mars, Jupiter, Saturn, Uranus, and Neptune.

Which planet is closest to the sun?

Which planet is farthest away?

Remember that sentence? It may help you.
My Very Elderly Mother Just Served Us Noodles.

4 What is the asteroid belt?

a) Something astronauts use to keep their trousers up in space

b) Space rocks that form a giant circle between Mars and Jupiter

c) The hole made on Earth when an asteroid hits the ground.

Answers

Page 4: 1) the largest planet is Jupiter 2) Neptune is very windy 3) Mercury is closes to the Sun

Page 5:

M	W	A	K	T	O	M	Y	M	P
J	I	P	N	U	R	A	A	E	M
U	S	Q	E	T	R	U	R	R	E
P	W	A	P	T	Y	U	M	C	S
I	S	E	T	U	S	O	N	U	P
T	F	A	U	U	P	L	H	R	T
E	P	J	N	T	R	T	M	Y	S
R	W	A	E	H	R	N	O	L	A
H	R	X	O	A	Y	U	G	R	E
U	W	Q	E	T	V	E	N	U	S

Page 6: 1) night 2) night 3) day 4) night

Page 7: The sun rises in the east

Page 8:

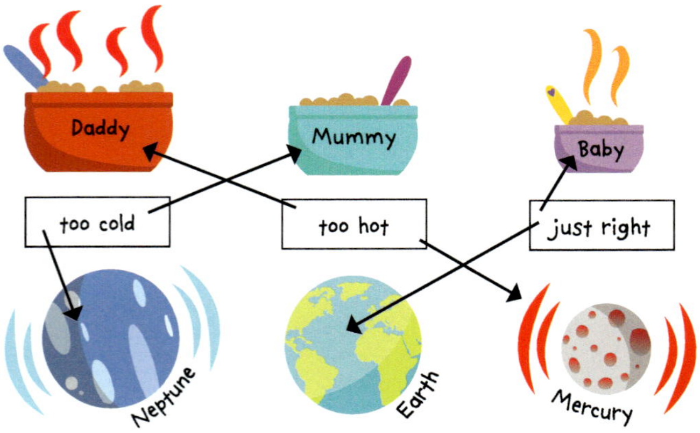

Page 9:

Page 10:

Page 11:

Page 12:

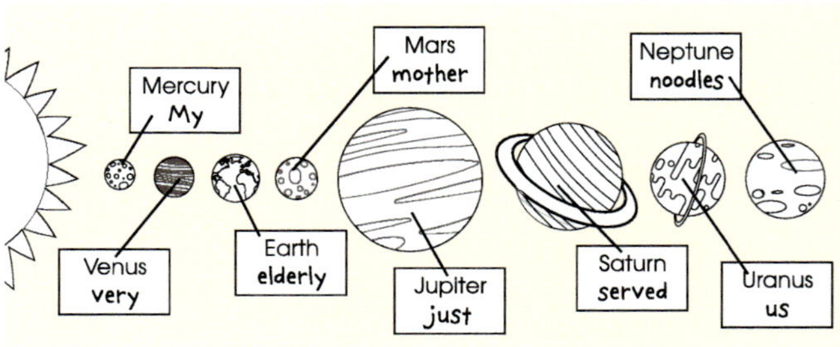

Page 13: 1 = Mercury, 2 = Mars, 3 = Venus, 4 = Earth, 5 = Neptune, 6 = Uranus, 7 = Saturn, 8 = Jupiter

Page 14:

Page 15: Venus, Rockets, Jupiter, Earth

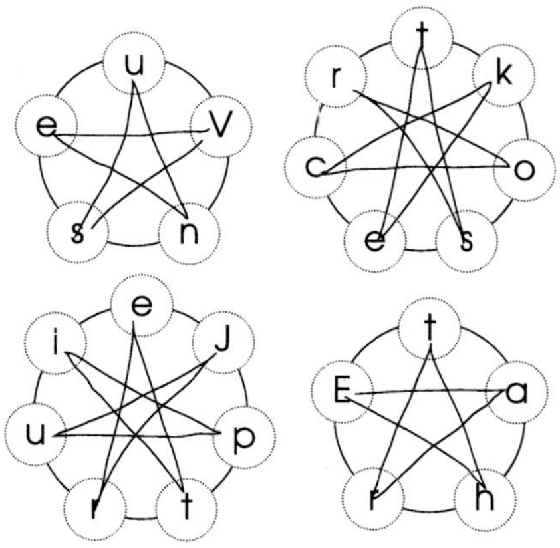

Page 17:

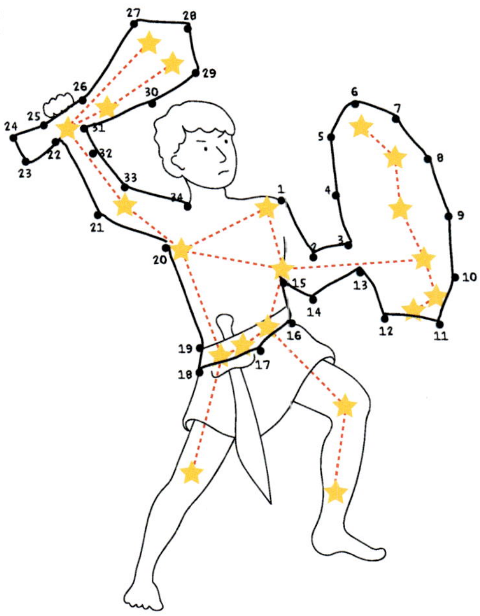

Page 21: 1) No, an asteroid is not bigger than a planet 2) Yes, comets are partly ice 3) Yes, a meteor is a burning meteoroid 4) a shooting star is another name for a meteor

The cross-out word is COMET

Page 22: B has the most stars. It has 9 and A has 5. Earth is circled.

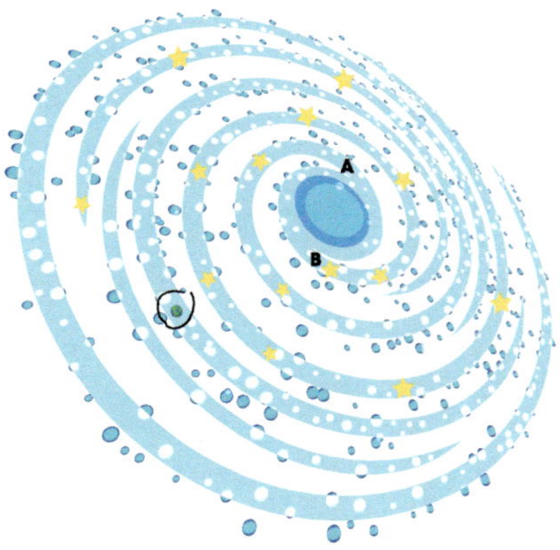

Page 23:

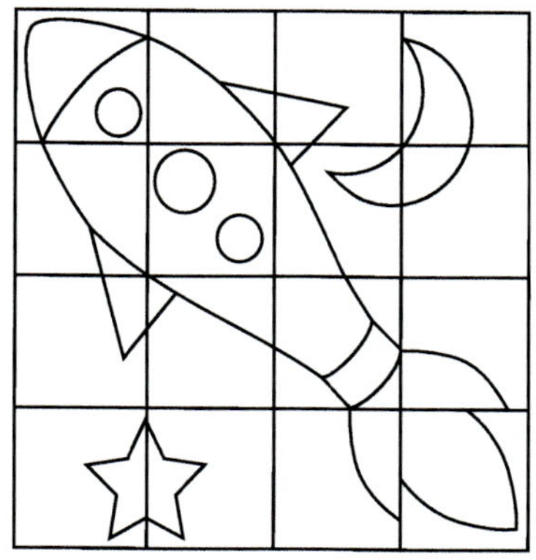

Page 24:

Page 28: Zob lives on Red Planet
Tok lives on Pink Planet
Mub lives on Blue Planet
Pib lives on Orange Planet

Page 29:

Page 30: 1) Spring 2) Summer 3) Fall 4) Winter

Page 31:

Page 32:

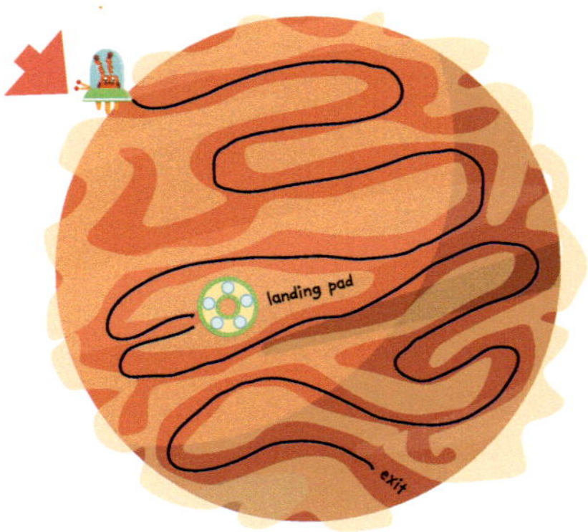

Page 33: 1) b - Jupiter has at least 79 moons 2) a - true, a day on Jupiter is shorter than on Earth

Page 35: The word is PLUTO

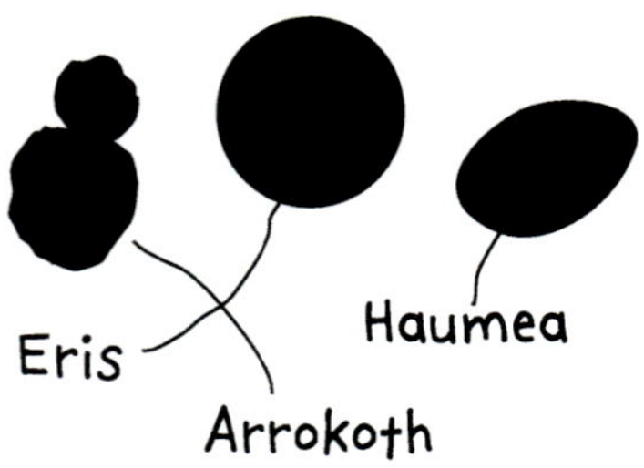

Page 36:

U	L	S	J	Z	O	W	Y	H	E
L	E	P	N	S	L	E	E	P	T
E	S	A	E	T	C	U	R	O	K
P	X	C	F	B	Y	U	D	N	E
F	S	E	T	W	S	O	I	U	K
O	D	S	R	U	P	R	H	R	L
O	P	H	N	C	D	T	M	T	S
D	W	I	M	H	I	N	E	A	O
B	S	P	A	C	E	S	U	I	T
U	L	Q	U	T	V	E	E	R	S

Page 39:

Page 40:

Page 43:

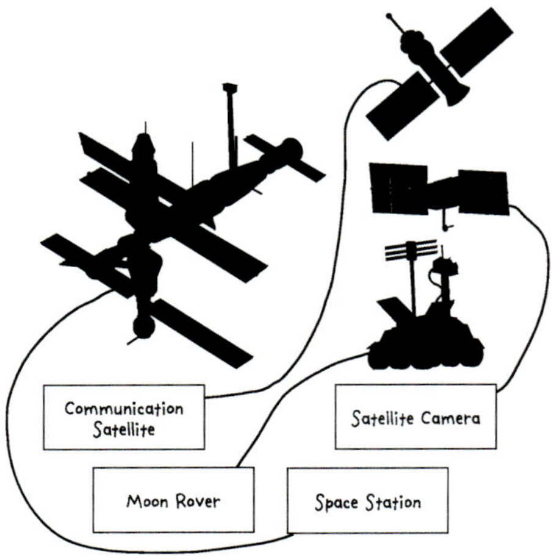

Page 44: 1) c - Gravity is an invisible force that pulls things to the center of planets. 2) a - Moonlight is actually sunlight bouncing off the moon. 3) Mercury is closest to the sun. Neptune is farthest from the sun. 4) b - The asteroid belt is a giant circle of space rocks between Mars and Jupiter.